Gospel's Story

Written by
Gary M. Best

Illustrated by
Leah-Ellen Heming

NEW ROOM PUBLICATIONS

Also by Gary M. Best

Fiction

Oliver Twist Investigates

Wuthering Heights Revisited

The Jacobite Murders

The Barchester Murders

Non-Fiction

Kingswood School: Continuity and Change

Charles Wesley

Shared Aims

Transforming Lives

The Seven Sisters

Susanna Wesley

A Tragedy of Errors: the story of Grace Murray

John Cennick: The Forgotten Evangelist

The Cradle of Methodism: a History of the New Room

His friends are helping the sick.
I travelled all over the country with John.
He wanted to tell everyone that
God loved them.

Here we are travelling on the road.
As he rode John used to read his **Bible**.
He loved all the stories about **Jesus**.
He trusted me to avoid any **dangers** in the road.

Have a look and you will see
just how **bad** the roads used to be
and some of the other dangers we faced.

Here we are at the **seaside**.
Have a look and you will see John is talking to **fishermen**.
Can you see the different types of **fish** they had caught?

John said he was God's fisherman.
He did not catch fish
but he captured people's **hearts**.
He asked people to **love** Jesus.

Here we are in a **town**.
You can see John is **speaking**.
John was not very tall. He stood on the steps so he could be seen.

Many people wanted to hear about God's love.
But some people tried to stop them hearing what John said.
Can you see what they are doing to make lots of **noise**?

Here we are at a **university**.
Students like to celebrate and have parties.
John said they should spend time helping the poor.
The Bible says the best way to have a good time
is to **help someone**.

Here we are in a **prison**.

Have a look.
Can you see why it was a
horrible place?

John is telling the prisoners
that God still **loves** them.
And that, if they say **sorry**,
God will **forgive** them.

LONDON JAIL ~

Here we are outside a **big church**.

John and his friends are **singing songs** to God.

Can you see why we're not inside the church?

Some people did not welcome **strangers**.

This made John very **sad**.

Here we are during a **riot**.
The people are cross and angry.

Some men are **attacking** John
and the house where we stayed.

Can you see how many **horrid**
things are happening?

John was always as brave as a **lion**.

Here we are in a **storm**.
We are getting very **wet**.

The road has turned to mud.
But God always kept John **cheerful**.

Here we are in the **snow**.
Sometimes I could not see where we were going.

The snow was very **deep**.
I **sank** into it up to the top of my legs.

John always trusted God to **guide us** to the next place.

Here we are at a **zoo** inside
a castle in Scotland.
Animals like **music**.

John is getting some men to
play music to the **lions**.

He told people to **look after**
all the animals and birds.

Here we are on a **boat**.
We had to cross a lake.

I was very **scared**.
John told me not to **panic**.

'Stay calm
and peaceful',
he said.
'God is with us.'

Here we are on a **mountain** in the mist.

We are in Wales.

For a time we could not find our way.

There were lots of **rocks** to fall over.

And **big cliffs** to fall down.

John was very **brave**.

Here we are visiting a **coal mine**.
Can you see the **pit ponies**?
They had to work under the ground.
So did the **miners**.

It was very hard work
digging for **coal**.
The miners **helped** each other.
John liked that.

**'I wish other people
were so good to
each other,'** he said.

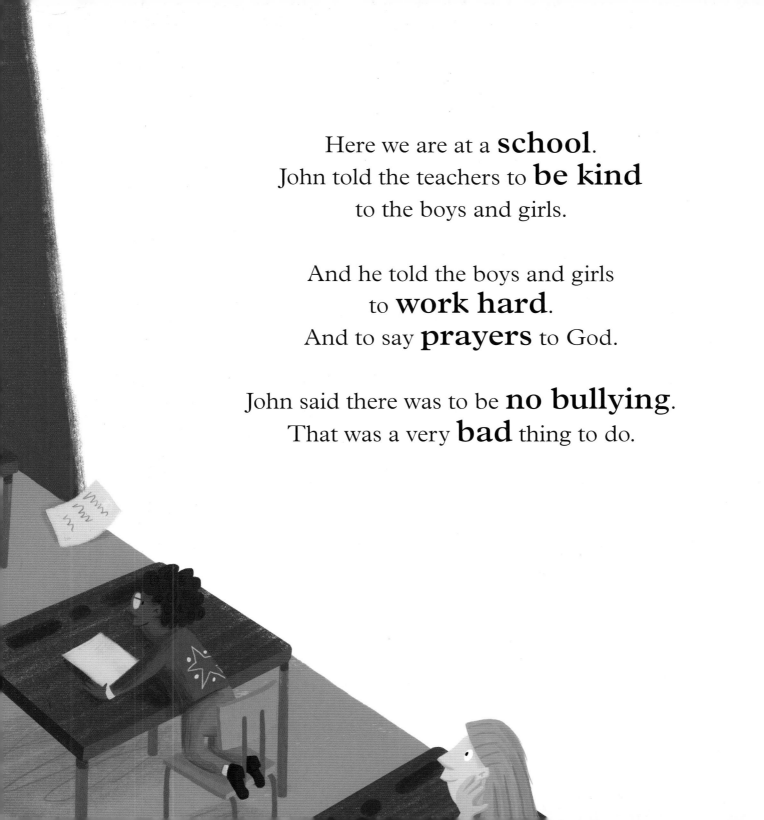

Here we are at a **school**.
John told the teachers to **be kind**
to the boys and girls.

And he told the boys and girls
to **work hard**.
And to say **prayers** to God.

John said there was to be **no bullying**.
That was a very **bad** thing to do.

This is the **statue** that was made of John and me.
Do you like it?
It's outside the **New Room** in **Bristol**.

But we never stayed there very long.
John soon said 'It's time to travel again.
Time to tell more people about God's love.
Time to tell more people to **be kind to each other**.'

NEW ROOM PUBLICATIONS

Gospel's Story
First published 2017

New Room Publications is an imprint of Tangent Books
Unit 5.16 Paintworks
Bristol BS4 3EH
0117 972 0645
www.tangentbooks.co.uk
Email: richard@tangentbooks.co.uk

ISBN 9781910089576

Author: Gary M. Best

Illustrations: Leah-Ellen Heming

Typesetting: Joe Burt (www.wildsparkdesign.com)

A CIP record of this book is available at the British Library.

Printed on paper from a sustainable source